A BIRDWATCHING GUIDE TO
THE ALGARVE

KEVIN & CHRISTINE CARLSON

ARLEQUIN PUBLICATIONS

ISBN 1 900159 00 7

First published 1995

Arlequin Press, 26 Broomfield Road, Chelmsford, Essex CM1 1SW
Telephone: 01245 267771
© Kevin & Christine Carlson

A catalogue record for this book is available.

CONTENTS

Red Rumped Swallow

Introduction

The southern part of Portugal from the Atlantic coast in the west to the Spanish border on the Ria Guidiana is known as the Algarve. It is roughly 150km as the crow flies, by 40km from Faro to the northern border with the Alentejo. The number of kilometers by road depends which route is taken.

The region can be divided into three, west of Faro to Cabo de S.Vicente and up the west coast to Odeceixe, then east of Faro to Vila Real de Santo Antonio on the border with Spain, and lastly the mountainous area running from east to west, inland from the coast, with the highest peak at Monchique.

The Algarve is well known as a pleasant place for holidays, a good climate, with many months of sunshine, and for its golf courses. During the summer, families arrive for swimming and sunbathing but may often wish to spend a day or two birdwatching.

In winter cheap holidays and weekend breaks are available from travel centres, and golf breaks are popular. It is also a good time for birdwatching, as many birds winter in the region, and many pass through on migration.

Indeed there is plenty to see for any person interested in nature, for a week or more, all the year round.

Most of the package holidays are centered around Faro, along the coast to Portimao, with some at Lagos to the west, and Monte Gordo to the east. The area around Faro is a good place to be based, as it is roughly halfway along the coast.

Topography

The westward region from Albufeira, called the "barlavento" (windward) has a rugged coastline with steep cliffs, sandy coves and short cliff top vegetation, due to the strong winds from the Atlantic.

Between Faro and Armãçao de Pêra is an area of pliocene sands forming long stretches of sandy beaches, backed by sand dunes, interspersed with woodlands of Stone (or Umbrella) Pines (Pinus pinea). Unfortunately this is the area of development, and although a number of estates are tastefully designed with low storey villas in attractive gardens, with a number of pine trees undisturbed, other small old fishing villages are being ruined by high rise concrete jungles.

Around Faro are large salt marshes, lagoons and sandy islands, spreading eastwards to Tavira called the "sotavento" (leeward) region. From the estuary at Tavira to Vila Real, the coastline becomes again sandy with sand dunes backed by extensive pine woodlands around Monte Gordo.

Behind the coastline is an area of cultivation to the foothills of the Serras. This is called the "barrocal" region, made up of jurassic limestone, dolomites and marl. The agriculture consists mainly of orchards of oranges, lemons, with almonds, figs and olives.

The Serras, Serra de Alcaria do Cume, Serra de Mú ou de Caldeirão, Serra de Monchique with the highest peak Foia (902m) ending in the west with the Serra do Espinhaco de Cão. In the Monchique range are the only syenite and foyaite rocks, the rest of the range are schists of carboniferous period.

Vegetation

The heathlands of the west coast are caused by the strong Atlantic winds stunting the vegetation and also closely cropped by sheep and cattle. Cistus, gorse, lavender, heathers and juniper grow, dwarfed in stature, with small alpine flowers of Hoop Petticoat Daffodils (Narcissus bulbocodium), Honeyworts (Cerinthe major) and the daisy-like flower, the yellow Asteriscus maritimus, amongst many others.

The marshlands and saltpans mostly occur around Faro. Wild asparagus, with its small spikey thorns, occurs along the banks of the saltpans. Rush and reed grow round the fresh water lakes and tall typha reedmace, locally called cane reed, is found along the river banks.

In the sandunes can be found salt resistant flowers such as the yellow Medicago marina, Allium subvillosum and Silene colorata, with large bushes of white broom and mimosa trees.

The fields across the central strip beneath the serras have patches of pretty Paper White Narcissus (Narcissus papyraceus) and the brilliant blue Barbary Nut (Iris sisyrinchium) beneath the orchards of pale pink almond blossom in early spring.

The pine woodlands, particularly around Monte Gordo have an undergrowth of several types of cistus, gorse, broom with the bright blue Gromwell (Lithospermum diffusum), as well as orchids and narcissi.

The vegetation of the serras varies considerably. So much has been deforested and eucalyptus planted as a quick growing source of wood, mostly for paper. Underneath these woodlands little grows as they thrive on poor soil taking any moisture present. This also applies to the planted forests of pines (Pinus pinaster).

The typical habitat "maquis" is of Holm and Cork Oaks, and in the wetter areas of the western serras, chestnuts. The undergrowth is of cistus of several varieties, the most prominent being the tall Gum Cistus (Cistus ladinfer) covering the hillsides with large dark centered white flowers in early summer. Long spiked Gorse (Genista hirsuta) brings bright yellow colouration mixed with the blue of the lavender (Lavandula stoechas) and the strange green form of lavender (Lavandula viridis).

Fine camellia trees are cultivated around Monchique with the creamy white flowered acacia (Acacia melanoxylon).

Accommodation

Most people will arrive with a package tour to Faro. There are immense numbers of hotels of all prices, all along the coast. There are innumerable villas to rent and now some bed and breakfasts advertised.

The best area to stay is around Faro, as this is the centre of the Algarve. The Quinta da Lago, Dunas Douradas and Vale do Lobo are very pleasant but expensive. Vilamoura near Quarteira is also good. All the small towns are a little over developed but give good accommodation.

For those driving down in motor caravans and caravans there are campsites, but not very many. Portugal is only just becoming geared to camping. A number of towns have sites, Monte Gordo, Fuseta, Olhão, near Armacão de Pêra, Portamão, Lagos, Luz, Figueira and two towards Sagres, all have reasonable camping facilities.

Travelling

Faro is the airport of the region, but some people may fly into Lisbon, hiring a car and driving down. The road is quite good and it takes about three hours, although in the height of summer it can be very busy.

It is really essential to have a car as the bird watching places are far apart. The only place where it would not be absolutely necessary, would be Quinta da Lago and Vale do Lobo where it is possible to walk, or hire a bicycle, to the river estuary and a hide by the lake.

Other people may wish to drive down from Calais or Boulogne across F rance and Spain, but this is a four-day drive. Another way is to take the boat to Santander in North Spain and drive down either through Spain, or much slower but very interesting, entering Portugal near Bragança and driving down the inland road through Guarda, Castelo Branco, Evora, Beja and then into the Algarve.

Winter breaks are worth considering, as package tours and fares can be very cheap and car hire reasonable, less than half summer prices. There are good numbers of wintering and migrant birds, with breeding starting early with White Storks on their nests, Hoopoes carrying food and even new hatched young on the backs of Great Crested Grebe parents by 1st February.

A good map of the Algarve is Hildebrand's Travel Map Algarve Southern Portugal 1:100,000. This also has a map of the western side up to Lisbon at 1:500,000 and a number of town maps Albufeira, Faro, Lagos and Portimão.

Azure Winged Magpie

Food

The Portuguese currency is the escudos. Travellers cheques and even better, the Euro-cheque, can be cashed in the many banks in all the towns and resorts.

Food is roughly the same price as the U.K., but fruit and vegetables bought at the local markets are cheap, with local baked bread and also wines and brandy. Fish is delicious, varied and plentiful, again best bought in the markets, but not very cheap except for fresh sardines.

There are innumerable mini and supermarkets. It is wiser to choose the smaller mini-market run by local people, than the large supermarkets in the resorts, that are very expensive.

Unfortunately it is difficult to find true Portuguese dishes unless you go inland. Fish is always excellent and in some restaurants bacalhau can be bought, a tasty dish made of dried cod, prepared in various ways. Another local dish is cataplana of pork, fish or chicken, made in a copper covered dish which is brought to the table. The pork with clams is well worth trying. A good meal, in the resorts, can be found for under 2,500esc up to over 5,000esc. Inland at a local restaurant meals would be half this price.

People and Customs

The Portuguese people are delightful. Most around the resorts speak English but even if they do not, with few words and signs, they are very helpful and pleasant.

Unfortunately like all European countries, these days there are thefts, but almost no violence. Never leave anything in the car, not even for a short while, especially cameras and binoculars. It is also wise to take care in locking the villas, even when unloading the car, out of sight of the villa.

There are a great many pottery shops, many with typical handmade pottery, in the local design of blue and white. Wooden furniture is interesting, but for most travellers, too large for flying. There are also local trades of jute made dolls and hand carved wooden toys. Their mats and carpets are good value, often made out of rags or hand woven. Lace making is still carried out with some beautiful table cloths etc.

Information

There has been very little written about the birds of Portugal. Many years ago in 1924 William C. Tait wrote the "Birds of Portugal" but this was mostly compiled from museum specimens. There was an early undated publication by Coverley "Bird notes-Portugal" and then in 1973 R. Cary produced "A Guide to Birds of Southern Portugal" but this was rather sketchy.

Since then nine volumes of "The Handbook of the Birds of Europe, The Middle East and North Africa" edited by S. Cramp et al (generally known as The Birds of the Western Palearctic) have been printed, but here again there are not very many references to Portugal.

In 1989 the Portuguese Atlas "Atlas das Aves que Nidificam em Portugal Continental" was compiled. There are only a few Portuguese ornithologists in the country and very much more research needs to be carried out for the birds in the atlas to be well covered.

A useful booklet is "An Atlas of

Great Spotted Cuckoo

Map 1. The Algarve.

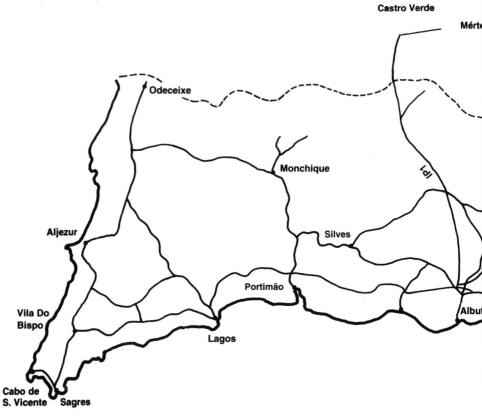

Wintering Birds in the Western Algarve" by Mark Bolton 1987, but again this only covers the western half from Armacão de Pêra in the winter.

Much of the information has been correlated by the authors from their studies and photography of the birds of Portugal since 1964, several months over this period having been spent in the Algarve.

There are a number of papers in Portuguese to which the authors have had access but most of these are on specific groups of birds, such as waterfowl, concerning the whole of Portugal.

There is no reference in print on the good birdwatching areas, so the authors hope this booklet will be of some help to those wishing to have a day birdwatching, or for those who wish to spend more time exploring the rich fauna and keen to pick up some of the Portuguese rarities.

Inland Tours (Map 1)

If there is a day to spare it is well worth driving to Castro Verde in the Alentejo, some 120km from Faro, to try to see Great and Little Bustard, Sandgrouse, as well as Black-winged Kite.

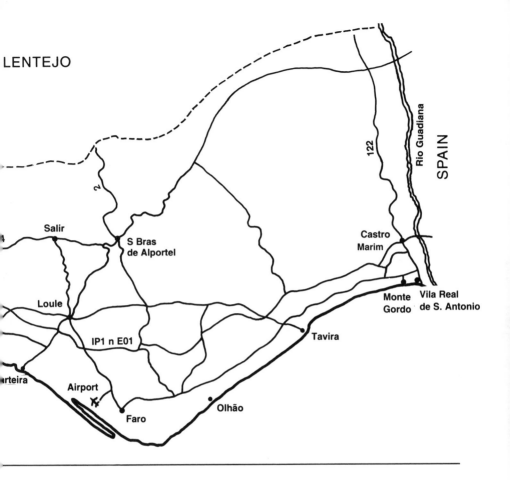

LENTEJO

SPAIN

Rio Guadiana

122

Salir

S Bras
de Alportel

Castro
Marim

Loule

Monte Vila Real
Gordo de S. Antonio

IP1 n E01

Tavira

rteira

Airport

Olhão

Faro

The best route is to take the 1P1 towards Lisbon turning off at Ourique to Castro Verde. From Castro Verde turn east towards Mértola.

On either side of the road are rolling plains and here is the chance to see the Great Bustard displaying to his females in April, the Little Bustard jumping and clicking in display in late April into May. Montagu's Harrier float over the grassland during summer. With luck Pintail and Black-bellied Sandgrouse can be seen in both summer and winter. Black-winged Kites sit in the trees, flying like silvery terns between the Cork or Holm Oak where they like to nest.

Great and Little Bustard gather in flocks during winter, roaming the hillsides. Crane also winter in the area and flocks as many as 500 occur on occasions.

There are numerous tracks turning off the main road and it is worth investigating these, as the birds wander about and it is difficult to pinpoint their displaying areas. On the north side of the road near Albernoa is a track leading to a deserted hamlet. A colony of Rollers nested in the holes in the walls of the crumbling buildings in 1989 and are probably still there, with a White Stork nesting on a chimney stack and Barn Owls in the buildings, plus thousands of rats!

Near Mértola amongst the olive groves is a good area for Rufous Bush Robin, if they have not been spotted in the Algarve, but they do not arrive until May.

John and Madge Measures of Quinta dos Almarjoes, Burgau, Lagos 8609 Tel. (082) 69152 take wildlife tours. They will organise both a visit to the Alentejo where they will try to find the mentioned birds plus more, and another tour along the coast to Castro Marim. They also take tours into Spain to the Coto Donãna.

Cabo de S.Vicente, Sagres and Buden (Maps 2 & 3)

Cabo de S.Vicente is the furthest western point of the Algarve. It is an area of vertical cliffs of limestone and sandstone rising to 150m. These cliffs are interspersed by sandy coves, a number inaccessable from land. It is interesting to watch the local fishermen angling from the top of the cliffs, casting their lines the 150m into the sea. It looks terrifying!

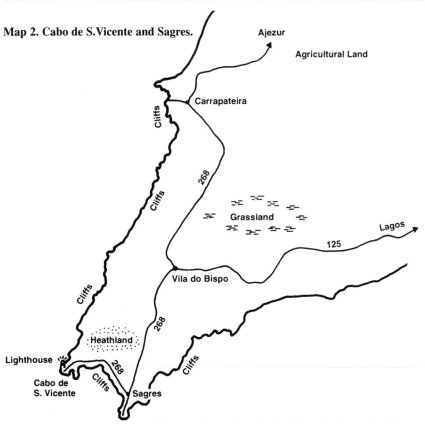

Map 2. Cabo de S.Vicente and Sagres.

The vegetation is of low heathland, and in spring the tiny Hoop Petticoat, the Honeywort and the yellow daisy-like flowers bring colour, with many other unusual plants. There is a lighthouse on the farest clifftop which can be visited. From just north of Odeceixe on the western coast, south to Cabo de S.Vicente and then along the coast to Burgau, is a protected area, which will mean that building will be under strict control.

The car can be parked by the side of the lighthouse. There are also organised excursions from many of the resorts. From here footpaths wander out to, and along the clifftops. On the road 268 to the lighthouse from Sagres, there are a number of pull-ins with footpaths to the top of the cliffs.

The bird specialities of the cape are Chough, Blue Rock Thrush, Alpine and Pallid Swift and Lesser Kestrel, all nesting on the cliffs. This is the only area in the Algarve where Choughs can be seen both in summer and winter. A few Alpine Accentors winter along the cliffs most years, but are difficult to pick out amongst the rocks and vegetation. Blue Rock Thrush, Kestrel, Jackdaw and Crow are resident and can be seen all the year round. Look carefully at the telegraph posts, as these are a common place to find the Blue Rock Thrush perching. When observed they are inclined to dodge behind the posts. Common Swifts join the other swifts in summer to nest in the crevices of the cliffs and so care should be taken to distinguish the three types. This is the best area for Alpine Swifts, the others can be found in several parts of the Algarve. Shags use the ledges on which to nest. Cormorants although they winter here, do not appear to breed.

In spring and autumn, the cape is renowned for the migrating birds, when innumerable warblers pass through, Willow and Garden Warblers, Nightingales, Tawny Pipits, Wagtails, Wheatears, Whinchat accompanied by Golden Oriole, Black Stork, Black Kite and Honey Buzzard are amongst many others.

Out to sea Cory's and Manx Shearwaters, Gannet, Puffin, Razorbill and Guillemot can be spotted. On the sea are often Common Scoter, with Skuas, Pomerine, Arctic and Great, making occasional appearances. In fact, during the autumn migration in particular, other rarities may turn up.

Inland from Sagres to Vila do Bispo, in the short vegetation Tawny Pipits, Short-toed and Lesser Short-toed Larks nest. The latter only found in this area. Watch out for Little Bustard especially in late April and May when they dominate their display ground by jumping, clicking and flashing their white wings to attract the females.

From Vila do Bispo the road north 268 has some good tracks on the west of the road, leading to the clifftops, where many of the previous cliff birds can be observed, also Black Redstarts that like the cliff ledges for nesting. Along the road towards Carrapeteira, in the fields in winter, gather flocks of Golden Plover, Lapwing and perhaps Stone Curlew.

From Carrapeteira to Ajezur still the 268, is more agricultural land, where Cirl Buntings reside, with Woodchat Shrike in good numbers, occuring in summer.

Map 3. Buden and Luz reedbeds and Lagos.

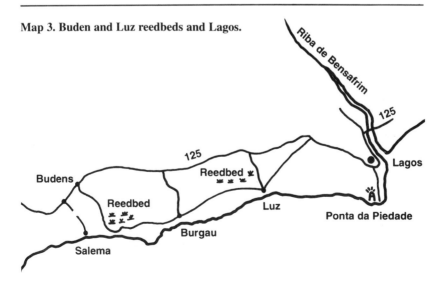

Driving back eastwards on the 125 from Vila do Bispo to Lagos, it is worth turning south at Budens to a smallish reed bed going down to the coast, where Reed and Great Reed Warblers, Waxbills and Little Bittern breed.

Another 10km on from the turning to Budens on the 125 is a turning to Luz. Here there is another small reed bed with tall typha reeds along the stream. During winter it is possible to see Penduline Tits on the cane reed, feeding on the seeds and insects. As many as 15 in a group have been recorded wintering there. In fact, other cane reed beds may well be worth investigating in winter, as observations have been few for this bird.

Lagos is a pleasant town to visit. Whilst there, a diversion to the lighthouse must be made, as in summer, beyond the lighthouse is a good colony of Cattle with some Little Egrets nesting on the rocks, of the rocky outcrop Ponte da Piedade.

Alvor Estuary and Quinta da Rocha (Map 4)

Driving eastwards from Lagos to Portimão on the 125, is a turning south to Quinta da Rocha. The turning is small and rather obscure, but it is opposite the lefthand or north turning signposted Mexilhoeira Grande. The lane is fairly narrow, soon passing over the railway line. Further along the lane, on the right is the A Rocha Christian Field Study Centre and Bird Observatory with a sign "Cruzinha" to it. This centre is open on a Thursday for foreign visitors. Its main purpose is for the education of the Portuguese in wildlife. It is understood that in future, it will be open more frequently for visitors. There is an interesting educational lecture room and the warden is very happy to help and suggest the best places to observe birds.

From this centre the road carries on to the estuary where it ends. On driving down, to the west are old saltpans ideal habitat for nesting Black-winged Stilt and Kentish Plover. On the east side of the road are meadows where, in winter, groups of Stone Curlew gather to feed. Beyond the meadows are more marshes with tracks leading down to them.

Probably one of the most interesting species of bird that can be seen in winter is the Bluethroat (white spot form). Examination of the salicornia may pick out a Bluethroat perching on top of the bushes, flitting from bush to bush.

The saltpans are excellent for spring, autumn and winter waders. Dunlin, Black-tailed Godwit, Ringed and Kentish Plover, Grey Plover, Lapwing, Redshank, Greenshank, Little Stint, Ruff and Little Egret with occasional Whimbrel, Curlew and Bar-tailed Godwit feed on the muddy saltpans and in the estuary at low tide. Many Grey Heron gather in winter feeding in the river and standing around resting in the scrubby marshland.

Along the western side of the saltpans the river Rio de Alvor flows into the estuary. At low tide many of the waders, particularly Redshank, Greenshank and Dunlin, feed, with several Little Egret.

There is a turning area at the end of the lane, where cars can be parked. It is possible, when the tide is low, to walk eastwards along the beach beneath the sandy cliffs. The thick vegetation growing down the cliffs makes excellent cover for migrating warblers. In winter there are many Chiffchaff and Sardinian Warblers, the latter breeding in summer along with Blackcap. Grey and Pied (white form) Wagtails feed along the coast in winter, whereas the Blue-headed Yellow Wagtail arrives in spring to breed. On the cliffs Black Redstart breed and can be seen in winter. Hoopoes fly over feeding on the grassland, in early spring, amongst the pretty White Paper Narcissi (Narcissus papyraceus), and nest in the old farm buildings in summer.

Great Spotted Woodpeckers and Little Owls live in the small copses, with Serin, Goldfinch and Greenfinch inhabiting the orchards and tree-lined lanes, joined by Woodchat and Great Grey Shrikes. Large numbers of Meadow Pipits spend the winter in the marshes and meadows feeding on the insects.

It is possible to walk round the banks surrounding the saltpans and estuary where good views of waders are obtained. Black-winged Stilt and Kentish Plover nest on the banks either on the mud or in low growing salicornia. As the area is being made a reserve, there may be some restrictions in the future during the breeding season.

Map 4. Quinta da Rocha, Alvor Estuary and Abicada.

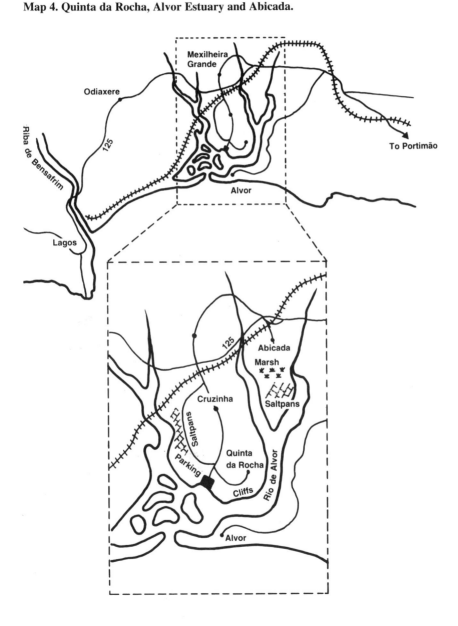

Abicada Marsh (Map 4)

When leaving Quinta da Rocha drop in to the Abicada marsh close by.

In recent years, with the drought, there is little water, but in a rainy year the marshes have innumerable pools amongst the salicornia where a large variety of waders can be seen. It is possible to take a track along the side of the river to the east of the marsh.

The turning to Abicada is the second turning south from the 125, after the turning to Quinta da Rocha, towards Portimão. Drive through the village, taking the first track to the right, as far as a farm building, past an old mill, which stands on high ground, where the car can be left. Follow any of the tracks across the marsh. Storks, Little Egret and Cattle Egret feed, with good numbers of the previously mentioned waders, plus Snipe and even Jack Snipe.

Portamão Harbour

A bird worth pursuing is the Purple Sandpiper. Although it is not supposed to migrate as far south as the Algarve, invariably a few birds can be found wintering amongst the groynes at the entrance to the Portimão harbour. They might well occur on other unexplored parts of the rocky coast.

Map 5. Armacao de Pera and Pera Marshes.

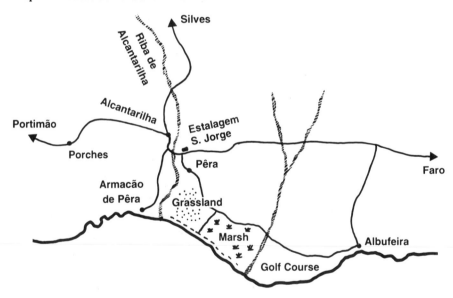

Armacão de Pêra Marshes (Map 5)

These areas lie about 18km west of Albufeira. The town of Armacão de Pêra is now an ugly development, but the river Riba de Alcantarilha runs along the eastern edge of the town and at the estuary, when the tide is out, a number of waders feed on the mud banks.

Much more interesting are the Pêra marshes. These are approached from the 125 route turning down south by the Estralagem S.Jorge. Drive through the village towards the beach. After the village, on a definite curve in the road, on the right-hand side, is a gravel track with a wide entrance, signposted to the beach, although the sign is not obvious. Take

14

the track through grassland scattered with fig trees, the marshes lying to the east, down to sand dunes and beach. Here the track divides west to the river at Armacão and east to the small river running through the marshes. Each track is drivable both summer and winter. Unfortunately part of the marsh to the east of the area has been made into a golf course.

In spring, autumn and winter this is an excellent place for waders and duck. Many Shovelers, a hundred and more, Mallard, Pintail and Pochard feed and rest amongst the vegetation. Little Grebe gather on the river in groups of 30+, with many Moorhen and Coot. Many Grey Heron can be seen fishing and resting on the banks. In summer Purple Heron may be present, but breeding has not been confirmed. Several Black-winged Stilt winter here as well as breed in summer. About half are first winter birds with their grey heads and necks. Black-tailed Godwit, Redshank and Dunlin feed in the shallows.

The hirundinidae hawk over the marshes and at times dozens of Crag Martins, Swallows and a few House Martins can be seen catching insects rising from the marsh.

Chiffchaff delight in alighting on the reeds and flying out to pick off the insects on and over the water. Possibly Bonelli's and Willow Warbler join them, as they pass through on migration. Even the rare wintering Sedge Warbler is sometimes present.

Take the car to the end of the track where the stream runs into the sea. Along the beach, groups of Sanderling race the waves and flying up and down the coastline, with luck, can be Sandwich, Common and even Little Tern. Occasionally a rarity such as Great Skua is distinguished from the innumerable immature Herring and Lesser Black-backed Gulls.

In summer many Black-winged Stilt and Kentish Plover nest on the raised ground of the marsh, which has generally dried out, with Sardinian Warbler nesting in the scrub and salicornia, along with the ubiquitous Fan-tailed Warbler in the deeper vegetation. Blue-headed Yellow Wagtails love the salicornia building on the ground under the bushes.

On the grassland can be heard but rarely seen, the tiny Quail. Short-toed, Crested and Thekla Larks love the sand dunes and short grass, to rear their young.

In early summer Gull-billed, Black and Whiskered Tern pass through often staying for several days resting and feeding. Little Terns come to fish throughout the summer, but breed further along the coast.

In spring the fine bushes of White Broom (Lygos monosperma) growing along the dunes and in the grassland, make a magnificent picture, often with Hoopoe ranging the grass, poking into the soil for insects and grubs.

Other migrants that occasionally pass through are Short-toed Eagle, Osprey, Little Stint, Green Sandpiper, Little Ringed Plover and Golden Oriole.

Parque Natural da Rio Formosa (Maps 6-9)

This park consists of 18400ha covering the area south of Faro, west to Quinta do Lago, and east to Tavira. It contains wetlands, marshes, saltpans and sandy islands.

The park headquarters are at Quinta de Marim just outside Olhão. Take the road east on the 125 from Olhão, and five km on your right is a petrol station. Turn down the next turning and a short way down on the left is the centre, soon after crossing the railway. It is not well marked but has large iron gates with a wide tarmac drive, but no obvious notice board. There is a small entrance fee.

The drive continues some distance past some buildings to a car park. The centre is worth a visit where maps can be collected indicating the walks around the saltpans. There is a walk around the reserve by the saltpans and through the scrub, along the dunes and the beach. A cool picnic area is situated under the pines.

Many waders winter here, and even more are seen on passage during migration. Black-winged Stilt and Kentish Plover are always present, and nest in summer. Little Terns and Collared Pratincole feed over the waterways in summer.

There is a bird of prey rescue hospital at the centre, one of only two in Portugal. It is

Map 6. Quinta do Lago.

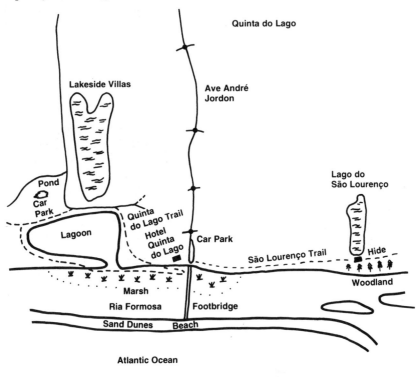

not at the moment open to the public, but they are hoping to put on show, in the near future, those who are too badly injured to be released.

The Parque Natural da Rio Formosa can be roughly divided into four sections, Quinta do Lago in the east, Faro and immediate marshes, the reserve centre, and the saltpans to the estuary at Tavira.

Quinta do Lago (Maps 6 & 7)

Quinta do Lago is about 18km west of Faro. From route 125 at Almancil, the road is well signposted south to Quinta do Lago, which is a very tastefully developed estate, with golf courses and a number of artificial lakes sometimes made from natural ponds. To the west of Quinta do Lago is Dunas Douradas running into Vale do Lobo, both well designed estates. The last two named are actually out of the reserve, but worth mentioning.

This is the very best area for finding Azure-winged Magpies, flying in groups through the Stone pines and feeding on the well watered golf courses, as well as raiding the communial dustbins. In summer they nest in the Stone pines in loose colonies.

Because of the Azure-winged Magpies, Great Spotted Cuckoo can be found. It is about the only place in the Algarve where they occur in summer. They parasitise the Azure-winged Magpies by laying one or two eggs in their nests. The incubation is shorter than the host, therefore the young outstrip the Azure-winged Magpie's young often to their detriment. They will parasitise Crows as well, but they are scarce in the Algarve. The

16

Plate 1. *The lighthouse at Cabo de S.Vicente the furthest western point of the Algarve. Blue Rock Thrush, Chough and Black Redstart can be found all the year round, with Alpine and Pallid Swift in summer. Alpine Accentor is a speciality most winters.*

Plate 2. *Heathland at Cabo de S.Vicente shows dwarfed vegetation. Tawny Pipit, Short-toed and Lesser Short-toed Larks nest in summer. The latter only to be found in this area.*

Plate 3. The cliffs at Quinta da Rocha. During migration many warblers rest and feed in the cliffside vegetation. Sardinian Warbler and Blackcap breed along with Black Redstart.

Plate 4. The PeraMarshes. An area of wet marshland with ponds and a small river running through. Haunt of many wintering duck, with Black-tailed Godwit, Redshank and Dunlin. Black-winged Stilt over winter and stay to breed in good numbers with Kentish Plover. Terns pass through on migration.

Plate 5. *The ponds at Dunas Douradas. These two ponds surrounded in reedbeds, are home to Purple Gallinule all the year and Little Bittern in summer, amongst Cetti's and Great Reed Warblers. Groups of Waxbill can also be seen.*

Plate 6. *Saltpans at Ria Formosa. Many waders and duck are found all the year. Little Tern and Pratincole nest on the sandy islands.*

Plate 7. *Lago de S.Lourenço, Quinta do Lago, an artificial lake surrounded by a golf course. A number of Purple Gallinule nest with Great Crested Grebe. Cetti's, Great Reed and a few Reed Warbler nest in the reedbeds. Many duck winter on the lake.*

Plate 8. *Saltpans at Fuseta. This area has saltpans in use and some abandoned, which are much enjoyed by many waders. Blue-headed Yellow Wagtails arrive in summer and with Sardinian and Fan-tailed Warblers nest in the surrounding vegetation.*

Great Spotted Cuckoo may well be found in other areas where Azure-winged Magpies nest but records are scarce.

Map 7. Quinta do Lago, Dunas Douradas and Vale do Lobo.

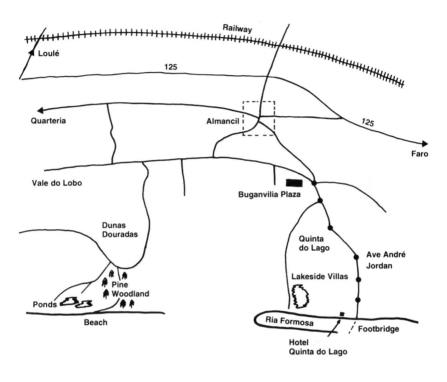

Dunas Douradas (Maps 6 & 7)

Just outside the reserve between Dunas Douradas and Vale do Lobo are two natural ponds, edged around with thick reed beds. It is possible to walk round the ponds, and a path meanders up between them. At least one pair of Purple Gallinule nest there, and if undisturbed, can be observed standing out on the edge of the reeds. Moorhen, Coot and Little Grebe nest in the reeds, also Water Rail, which are difficult to see but easily heard with their grunting and squealing calls. Great Reed Warblers like the tall cane reeds, nesting in May to June. Almost always a Kingfisher can be observed sitting on a branch over the water waiting for fish. Parties of Waxbill frequent the reedy areas.

In winter Shoveler, Tufted, Mallard and Pochard shelter in the ponds. Cattle Egret and Little Egret are generally present and Buzzard and Kestrel hunt around the area. It is intriguing to watch literally dozens of Chiffchaff chasing out over the water to catch the insects flying over, and scooping them up from the surface of the water, then flying back to perch on the reed stalks. Cetti's Warblers can be heard and sometimes seen, also breed in the tall vegetation. It is worth sitting for an hour or so watching as it is possible to see the elusive Little Bittern that breeds in the reeds and occasionally over winters.

Many Meadow Pipits, Crested and Thekla Larks, with groups of Goldfinch feed on the

21

seeding plants and insects on the dunes, with Crested and Thekla staying to nest. Black Redstarts and Grey Wagtails are often present in winter.

Quinta do Lago has produced a useful booklet on the area of the estate, obtained from the reserve centre and the hotels.

To get there, after passing the Buganvilla Plaza shopping centre, take the road through the archway and turn west at the first roundabout marked Lakeside Villas. The road passes a golf course on the west and ends in a parking area in front of the lagoon. On the east side of the road are the villas and a large artificial lake, but little other than gulls and coot use it, as it is a recreational area.

An hour or more can be spent looking out over the water of the lagoon. It is best early morning or late afternoon, otherwise the sun is south making observation difficult. There is a fish farm and mollusc beds in the Rio Formosa estuary, as well as saltpans. A raised pathway along the banks, goes out across the marshes eventually leading to the bridge over the estuary to the beach. On this walk Bluethroat (white spot form) can be seen flitting across the salicornia in winter. Spoonbill rest on the islands, with Little Egret and Grey Heron wading in the water feeding.

The best time to see the waders is during the spring and autumn migration, but also a number stay to winter. Some stay all the year round so there is always something to see. Hundreds of Dunlin, Black-tailed Godwit, Redshank, Greenshank, Ringed Plover are always present, with rarer Curlew, Whimbrel, Curlew Sandpiper, and Little Stint. Many duck including Gadwall, Pintail, Shoveler are in good numbers. Groups of Little Grebe form rafts of 30 or more, with hundreds of Coot. A few Black-winged Stilt are always present. Caspian Tern frequently winter along the waterways, as do Sandwich and a few Common Tern. Little Tern can be seen fishing in summer, but nest out on the islands.

Lago de S.Laurenco

Returning to the first roundabout, take the main road through the estate, the Av.André Jordan, crossing over a number of roundabouts to a parking place just past the Hotel Quinta do Lago.

Across the estuary is a long footbridge to the beach. Many birds can be watched from the bridge. In summer this becomes very busy, as it is the only access to the sea from the estate.

On the beach Sanderling run along the tide, and Kentish Plover may still nest in the sand dunes during the summer.

By the car park grow aloes and at the right time of the year when they are in flower, Chiffchaff have been seen feeding from the nectar like sunbirds.

Eastwards from the car park is a marked trail running along the side of the golf course to the left (beware of the golf balls!) and the marshes to the right. Many waders feed on the mud flats at low tide, Redshank, Greenshank, Dunlin, Black-tailed Godwit with sometimes Green or even Wood Sandpipers. The islands in the estuary are roosts in winter, for very many Black-headed, Lesser Black-backed Gulls. Often groups of Sandwich Terns, with a few Common Tern occupy one end to roost, away from the gulls.

In summer some non breeding waders remain, but from October to April are the best months for wader watching.

The trail is 2.3km return to the hide erected looking over the Lago de S.Laurenço, an artificial lake surrounded by the golf course. The hide overlooks the lake and faces north, so any time of day is possible for observation. There are a number of Purple Gallinule (and even some of the smaller ponds on the golf course hold a pair) that wander out from the reeds and onto the golf course to feed. Many Coot, Moorhen and Little Grebe nest in the reeds and at least one pair of Great Crested Grebe. These birds have been seen as early as the 1st February with new hatched young on their backs. Black-necked Grebes have been reported as nesting by the lagoon.

Several species of duck winter on the waters, Shoveler, Pochard, Tufted, Wigeon and Pintail are always present, as well as the resident Mallard.

The status of the Purple Heron is at present rather problematic. Undoubtedly they can be seen feeding in the estuary and in the lagoon in summer, but there is no recent evidence of nesting in the locality, although at one time they bred in Ludo.

Cetti's Warbler, Great Reed and occasionally Reed Warblers breed. Little Bittern and Water Rail, both secretive, find the reed beds suitable nesting areas. Little Tern can be seen feeding over the lake, but nest out on the sandy islands. During migration both Black and Whiskered Tern pass by, spending a day or so feeding.

There are pine woods of Stone Pine, with Carob Trees (Ceratonia siliqua) and an undergrowth of gorse, cistus, and the European Fan Palm (Chamaerops humilis). These lie beyond and to the seaward side of the hide. Sardinian Warblers, Golden Oriole and Woodchat Shrike inhabit the scrub and pine woods, also Little Owl, Hoopoe and more Azure-winged Magpies. Some tit boxes have been put up in the trees for the Great and Blue Tit, and occasionally Crested Tits are present. Short-toed Treecreepers can be heard and seen running up the tree trunks. Hawfinches are present along with common finches, Chaffinch, Greenfinch and Serin.

Anyone interested in reptiles might care to look carefully in the vegetation of the dunes and through the pine woods, where, with luck the rare Chameleon (Chamaelo chamaeleon) can be found early morning or late afternoon, swivelling their eyes to find insect prey.

Ludo

Ludo estate is not part of the reserve and it is almost impossible to get permission to enter. The authors were disappointed in the estate when last they made a survey in 1986. No Purple Heron or Little Egret colonies were there, but the lagoon held ten pairs of Purple Gallinule. In 1972 and 1973 there was a large colony of both Purple Heron and Little Egret, with some Little Bittern nesting in the reeds. Since then, unfortunately, the reed beds have become overgrown with tamarisk and salix, which may have been the reason for their desertion.

The estate has been mentioned as it is still quite often referred to by birdwatchers, but as far as can be ascertained, the estate is still strictly private.

Faro

The tracks to the saltpans and marshes round Faro are a little difficult to find. It is worth trying the saltpans behind the airport. Take the road past the airport to the beach and immediately after the perimeter fence, there is a track east. Drive down this track inspecting the saltpans to the right for waders, Little Egret and Black-winged Stilt.

The saltpans either side of the road to the bridge leading to the beach, are worth a stop. There are a few pull-ins where the birds can be watched from the car.

The next stop is the sewage works. To get to them turn off the road to Monte Negro before the airport. In the town turn south through Marchil, the sewage works are at the end of the road. The works are enclosed with chainlink fencing but good views can be obtained from the track, and there is a walking track across a wooden bridge to the marsh. In summer Little Tern feed over the area, with Black and Whiskered and Gull billed Tern passing through, and in winter there are a number of duck and Little Grebe. Look out for Black-necked Grebe amongst the latter.

From the Faro harbour it is possible to hire a boat which can sail around the islands where Little Tern, Collared Pratincole and Little Egret nest as well as Kentish Plover.

Map 8. Ria Formosa Reserve and Fuseta Saltpans.

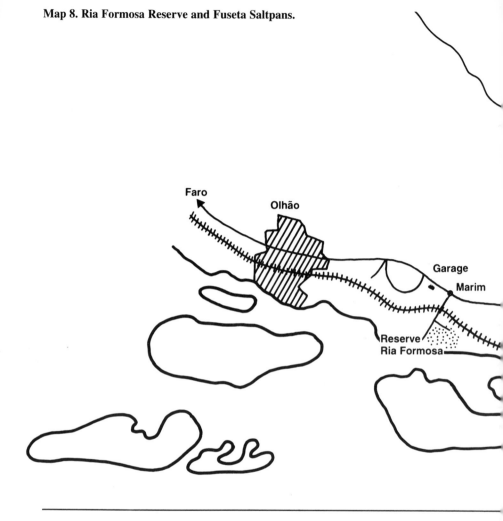

Saltpans of Olhão and Fuseta (Map 8)

Halfway between Faro and Olhão on the 125 route, there is a radio mast in an enclosed area. On the Faro side is a track running along the side of the enclosure, where a colony of Collared Pratincole can be seen nesting in the summer.

Driving on eastwards through Olhão and the road to the Reserve centre, on the 125, there are many turnings to the right which go down to the saltpans and marshes through unspoilt fishing villages.

Three turnings after the one signposted to Fuseta, turn opposite a pottery shop. This lane goes down to some good saltpans with a fish farm to the south of them. The track eventually runs down the east side of the estuary, with Fuseta on the other bank, into some works.

Greater Flamingo often rest in these saltpans in winter, and many remain in summer. The pans hold the usual waders, with many Dunlin, some Black-tailed Godwit, Green-

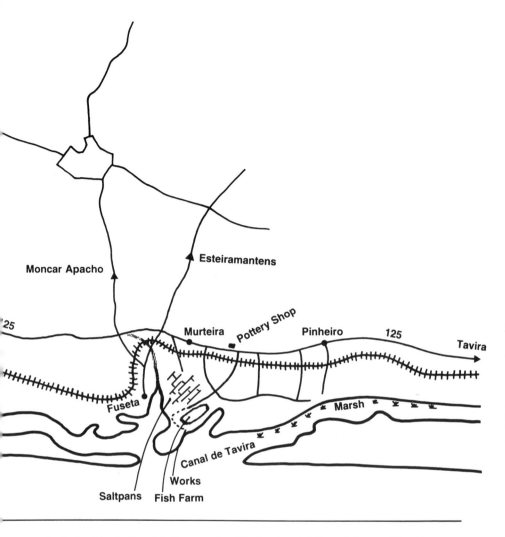

shank, Redshank, Kentish Plover, a few Black-winged Stilt and Avocet. The drier pans have Oystercatcher, Turnstone and Grey Plover. Any waders may turn up so it is worth examining them with care. An hour or more can be spent watching either from the car or walking around the banks of the pans. Grey Herons and White Stork stand around resting or wade through the water fishing.

The saltpans alter from year to year, as some are taken out of production whilst others are flooded for further salt extraction. Take a little time to look for the best pans with not too much water.

The fish farm lying to the seaward side of the pans hold screaming, fighting gulls, squabbling over fish scraps. Examine these carefully for amongst the usual Black-headed, Lesser Black-backed and Herring Gulls are often Mediterranean and Little Gull.

In summer Black-winged Stilts and Kentish Plover nest, and in the scrub around the pans Sardinian Warblers, Fan-tailed Warbler and Blue-headed Yellow Wagtails also breed.

25

Map 9. Tavira Saltpans.

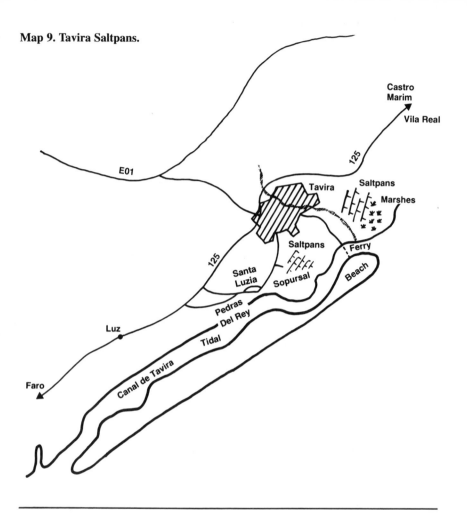

Tavira (Map 9)

Tavira is a pleasant town worth exploring. A ferry runs from the quayside to the beach, but is very crowded in summer. It is the hottest part of the Algarve with temperatures well into the high eighties. There is a small but very old castle to explore with Swift and Pallid Swift nesting.

To get to Tavira, either take the direct route off the 125 straight into the town, or much more interesting, turn off the 125 at Santa Luzia and follow the canal road into Tavira. At low tide there are many waders, Oystercatchers and Turnstone particularly like the mud flats, also Little Stint, Curlew Sandpiper, Sanderling probe in the mud. Before entering Tavira there are saltpans on the south of the road. At the works with a sign Sopursal, the car can be left at the gate, or even permission to drive the car in, can be obtained, but be careful to leave by 5.30 pm, when the gates are closed. The saltpans are very good for all the waders already mentioned.

On driving through the town to the ferry, saltpans are on either side of the road. A stop to examine these can be rewarding.

26

Map 10. Monte Gordo and Castro Marim.

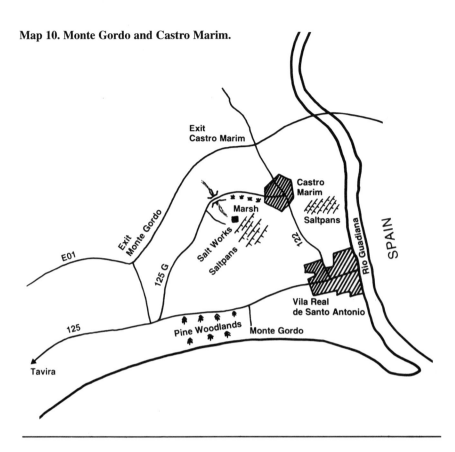

Reserva Natural do Sapal de Castro Marim and Vila Real de Santo António (Maps 10 & 11)

Castro Marim lies on the west side of the Rio Guadiana on the Spanish border. Due south is Monte Gordo, a resort, and to the south west Vila Real de Santo António on the river. There is a ferry carrying vehicles across to Spain, and recently a bridge has opened north of Castro Marim into Spain.

The town can be appoached from 125 route from Tavira, or from the new E01, turning off either at the exit to Monte Gordo, and then immediately turning north again after joining the 125 to Castro Marim on the 125G, or leaving the E01 at the exit to Castro Marim before the Spanish border, and entering the town from the north on the 122.

The reserve was established in 1975 and comes under the jurisdiction of the Ria Formosa Reserve. It consists of 2,000+ha, mostly saltpans either abandoned or in production, with marshy land around.

In the middle of the town is the old castle standing on high ground overlooking the reserve. The headquarters of the reserve is situated within the castle. Cars can be taken up to the foot of the castle and left, from here the headquarters are signposted. It does not open until at least 10.30am. Information and pamphlets are obtained here, showing the boundaries and footpaths of the reserve. Often in the grounds of the castle are White Storks recovering from various injuries. This gives a good opportunity to observe these birds at very close quarters, as they become quite tame.

27

The reserve is renowned for its wintering Greater Flamingo which can number 500+ at times. A number of non-breeders remain throughout the year. There is one report of a small juvenile with parent, but breeding is unconfirmed and needs further investigation.

The other speciality is the colony of breeding Avocets. There is only one other known breeding area of Avocets in Portugal, which is near Lisbon. There are always good numbers in winter feeding in the saltpans.

Many waders and waterfowl winter in the saltpans and pass through on migration. Twenty-three different species have been recorded, with good numbers remaining throughout the year.

One of the best areas for birdwatching is by the salt works. When approaching Castro Marim from the 125 turning north on the 125G, there is a wide gravel track just before a bridge. Take this track and park by the iron gates into the works. Be careful not to block the entrance or the track outside.

Map 11. Castro Marim Salines with tracks.

On the right or south of the track is a meadow which becomes flooded in winter but dries out in summer. Black-winged Stilts, Redshank, Black-tailed Godwit, and Ruff feed here with a few Snipe, possibly Jack Snipe and Common Sandpipers. Watch out for Green and Wood Sandpipers dropping in to feed during migration and even during the winter. Gulls both Black-headed and Herring roost, bathe and squabble, while White Storks sit around resting.

On the left or north of the track are muddy wet marshes where Grey Heron and large numbers of White Stork rest, whilst waders feed in the small pools. Pied Wagtails (white form) are plentiful in winter with Corn Buntings and Stonechats sing from the tops of the salicornia.

Looking right across the marsh to an olive grove, there are a large number of White Storks nests built low down on olive trees. Castro Marim is the very best area for White Storks in the Algarve. Even as early as January pairs repossess their nests, and can be

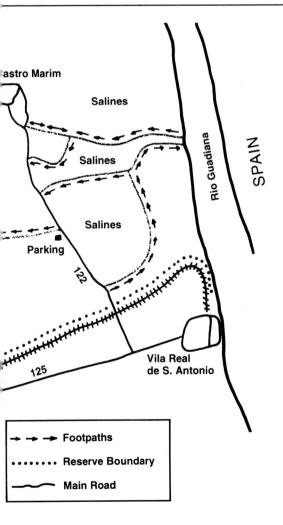

29

spotted standing on the edge starting to rebuild. There are at least a dozen occupied nests with further ones on surrounding buildings in and around the town.

Entering the gates of the saltworks on foot, there are footpaths along the banks of the saltpans. The saltpans can also be entered by a track leading off the 122 south of Castro Marim. The car can be parked at the entrance and a short distance along is a bird observatory. It is in these saltpans the Greater Flamingo can be found, a magnificent sight of pink plumage, pink and black bills, with red and black wings seen in flight. Amongst these are a fair percentage of juveniles, lacking the pink colouration, being a dirty white.

The waders include Ringed and Kentish Plover, Grey and Golden Plover, Black-tailed Godwit in very large numbers, a few Bar-tailed Godwit, Redshank, Spotted Redshank, Greenshank, Ruff, Little Stint and huge numbers of Dunlin, Black-winged Stilt, Avocet and Little Egret feed in the shallows. Many of the waders will stay as late as May.

Outside the saltworks take the track along the edge of the dyke past the farm. A little distance along is an extensive wetland to the right or west of the track. In winter when there is much water, large numbers of waterfowl feed and rest amongst the vegetation and pools, including Shoveler, Pintail, Teal and Gadwall as well as the resident Mallard.

In summer the wetlands dry out but water remains until the height of summer. Good numbers of waders remain joined by Spoonbill, Avocets and Black-winged Stilts. The latter have probably the largest nesting colony in the reserve, in Portugal. Avocets also breed on the mud flats. Several terns fly over feeding, with Little Tern breeding in the area. Black and Whiskered Terns fly over also Sandwich Terns, all on their way north. Little and Mediterranean Gull pass through on migration, including Slender-billed Gull which has also been recorded. Occasionally Glossy Ibis have been spotted, that have strayed from their breeding grounds in Eastern Europe.

Of the small birds, Spectacled Warblers breed in fair numbers in the salicornia and scrub, with a number of Blue-headed Yellow Wagtails and the ubiquitous Fan-tailed Warbler.

On the drier mud banks large numbers of Kentish Plover and Black-winged Stilt breed, lining their nests with tiny shells. Little Tern and Collared Pratincole have colonies generally on the other salines east of Castro Marim.

The saltpans on the east of the 122 road are worth visiting, as amongst the usual waders, a rarer species may be spotted. There are several walking tracks leading off the 122 south of Castro Marim. Even in May to June there are plenty of waders about, most in breeding plumage, but it is presumed they are non-breeders, as breeding will be well under way in their northern haunts.

Stone Curlew can be found on the drier agricultural land, and Montagu's Harrier can generally be seen flying over the area, but tend to breed further north of Castro Marim in larger areas of agricultural land.

Monte Gordo

Monte Gordo is an ugly resort, but surrounded by Stone pine woods with an undercover of white broom, cistus, and in early spring pretty Hoop Petticoat Daffodils as well as orchids. Plenty of tracks give access to these woods.

In this habitat the small woodland birds thrive. Short-toed Treecreepers, Crested Tits, Great Grey Shrike and Woodchat Shrike, Melodious Warblers and Serin are some of the more unusual birds occurring in summer, with the first three wintering as well. Buzzard and Black Kite nest in the pines.

Map 12. Azinhal.

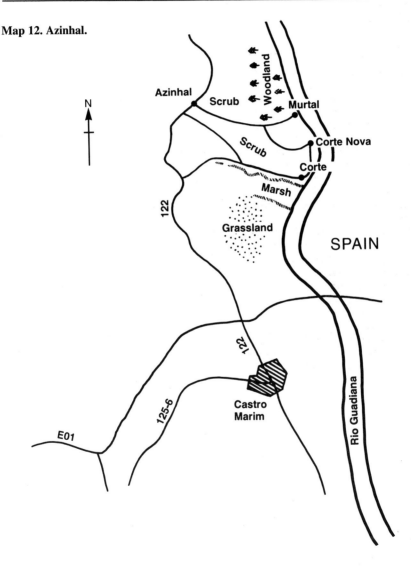

Azinhal (Map 12)

Eight kilometers north of Castro Marim on the 122 is Azinhal, where lies an oak and scrub woodland with some marshland. A road runs due east of the town to Murtal on the river, with tracks leading off the road to the south. Crested Tit, Woodchat Shrike and a few Orphean Warbler nest in the trees. Rufous Bush Chat can be found in the scrub, but not until late May, whilst Wood Lark prefer the open spaces under the trees. In the wetter areas Nightingale and Cetti's Warbler are present, with Great Reed Warbler in the reed beds.

On the drier grassland are Little Bustard and Stone Curlew, with Montagu's Harrier in the agricultural land.

Swallows and House Martins are common, with Red-rumped Swallows nesting under the culverts. Hoopoes are plentiful and Bee-eaters are often seen flying overhead with their characteristic calls, hawking for insects.

Map 13. River at Martim Longo.

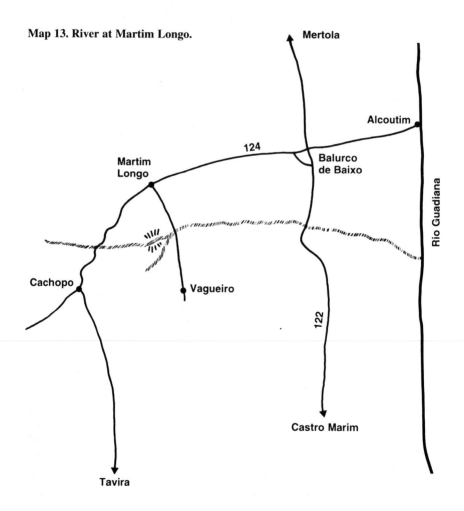

Martim Longo (Map 13)

Take the road north on 122 towards Alcoutim. On the left or west, 33km from Castro Marim, take the 124 before Alcoutim signposted to Martim Longo 25km. In this village there is a small turning south to Vaqueiros, which crosses a river. Park the car and explore the river beds. In summer much of the river dries up, but in winter it holds water. On the west of the road is a small river with a ravine. Blue Rock Thrush, Rock Bunting and Black-eared Wheatear can be found. The other side of the road to the east, the river widens and on the shingle banks Little Ringed Plover nest, Common Sandpiper feed along the edge with Grey Wagtails.

Further towards Vaqueiros are dry grasslands and agricultural land with Little Bustard, Stone Curlew, Montagu's Harrier and larks, Crested, Thekla, Short-toed and Calandra.

The Serras

The range of hills inland from the coast, are made up of schists of the carboniferous period. Then separating them from the limestone band south, is a band of tertiary sandstone and conglomerates.

Unfortunately much of the serras natural vegetation has been destroyed with large areas deforested and replanted with eucalyptus and pines (Pinus piaster), whilst other areas are being farmed. Where the natural vegetation remains grow Cork and Scrub Oak with an undergrowth of several varieties of cistus, the dominant tall Gum Cistus (Cistus ladanifer) with their large white flowers and dark centres, making a spectacular sight in early summer. Heathers, gorses and lavender bring reds, whites, yellows and blue to the hills. In early spring patches of tiny yellow narcissi and orchids can be found in suitable areas, with the tall white asphodels waving in the breeze.

The range from east to west, consists of Serra de Alcaria do Cume in the east, then Serra de Mú ov de Caldeirão, followed by the Serra de Monchique with its highest peaks of Foia (902m) and Picota (744m). Lastly to the west before the coast, is the Serra do Espinhaco de Cão.

Monchique (Map 14)

The most obvious and well known serra to explore is Monchique. The town of Caldas de Monchique is an old Roman watering place with refreshing springs, old streets and squares well worth a visit. Driving on up the mountain to Monchique, the road 266-3 is taken to the highest peak Foia. Monchique has become increasingly tourist orientated, with many new houses built on the hillside. The road up to Foia is easy but twisting and at the top is a weather station, satellite dishes and a very ugly restaurant. Even so it is worth exploring the walking tracks from the top.

On a clear day Golden Eagle may well be spotted. Certainly Buzzard are common, and Booted Eagle should be looked for. Blue Rock Thrush occur and in the scrub vegetation Rock Bunting and Dartford Warbler.

A very pleasant run is to take the road 267 west to Marmelete, after Caldas de Monchique and before Monchique. This road runs more or less in the foothills of the range. The views are interesting and the little villages appear along the route one after the other. It is preferable to take one of the roads off to the right, signposted to villages such as Almarjunhos and Covao. These wander up through the foothills where Buzzard are common, Short-toed Eagle, Booted Eagle and Black Kite should be seen, and with luck Goshawk and Sparrowhawk. It is possible also to see Bonelli's Eagle but it is rare. Eagle Owl breed in remote regions, but are unlikely to be seen, although they may be heard at

Map 14. Serra de Monchique.

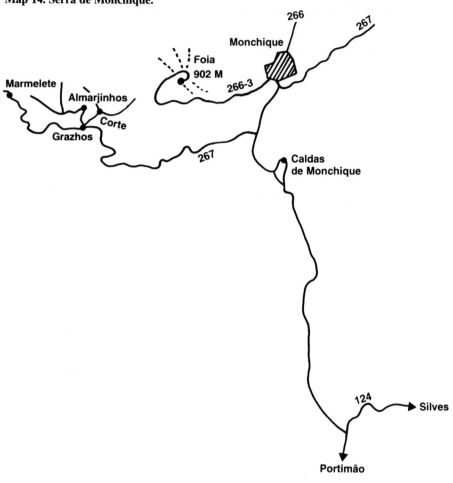

dusk. Red-necked Nightjars can be put up from dry areas, and are one of the few birds to enjoy eucalyptus forests. All three Woodpeckers, Green, Great and Lesser Spotted breed in the mixed woods and can be heard and seen all the year round. Wrynecks can also be found, but they are not common. In the woodlands Crested Tit, Short-toed Treecreeper and Nuthatch breed. Crested Tits in Portugal like Scrub and Cork Oaks and Silver Birch, and not pines as in Scotland. Firecrests occur in winter, with a few Goldcrest, so care must be taken to distinguish the two. Some reports claim the Firecrests breed in the region, but more investigation needs to be carried out.

Sardinian Warblers are common, but Dartford and Subalpine Warblers also breed in the scrub, therefore close examination is essential to differentiate them. Rock Buntings are a good bird of the area. Little Owls sit around in trees and on posts during the day. Scops Owls are scarce but do occur, being nocturnal they are generally found sitting close against the trunks of trees. The serra is a little disappointing as much of the hillside has been cleared and in many areas eucalyptus and pines planted. Other hillsides are being used for agriculture.

Map 15. Odelouca Valley and Silves.

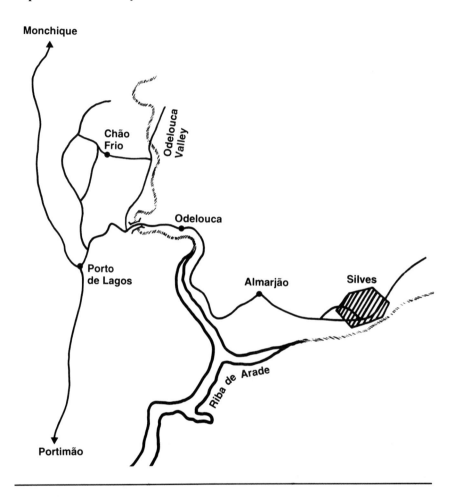

Odelouca valley (Map 15)

On the way down from Monchique to Portimão, turn eastwards on the 124 at Porto de Lagos to Silves to explore the Odelouca valley. The second turning left, before the bridge, turn north along a minor road towards Chão Frio, which starts by running along the river. Azure-winged Magpies frequent the riverside. Before Chão Frio the road forks, taking the right-hand track leads back again to the river. There on the shingle islands breed Little Ringed Plover, Bee-eaters in the sandy banks, with possible Kingfisher. Little Egrets wade in the shallows and Common Sandpiper run along the edge with their bobbing action, whilst Grey Wagtail stand on rocks darting out for insects. The scrub around have Dartford

35

and Subalpine Warblers breeding and Melodious Warblers in the bramble. There are further tracks running up beside the river, which are worth walking if time permits.

A stop should be made at Silves, once the capital of the Algarve, which has a splendid castle and church. Swifts, Pallid and Alpine can be seen with many House Martins. Lesser Kestrel, although scarce, nest in the old buildings.

Map 16. Serra de Mú ou de Caldeirão.

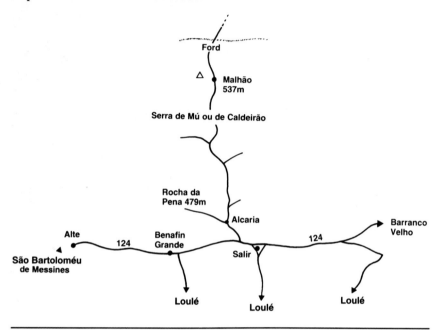

Serra de Mú ou de Caldeirão (Map 16)

The Serra de Mú ou de Caldeirão which lies north of Loulé, is preferred by the authors. There is a new fast road to Salir, although the road out of Loulé is difficult to find. The other route to Salir on the 124, turns west out of Loulé on 270. After 6km turn north to Alto Fica and Benalim Grande. At first there are many citrus orchards but soon after turning off the 270 the area becomes stony with scrub oaks and scrub undergrowth. Sardinian, Dartford and Subalpine Warblers occur. Watch out for Melodious Warbler, and the Olivaceous Warbler as this is one of the few areas where they can be found.

When reaching the 124 turn west to the very attractive old cobbled village of Alte. It is well worth a visit for a break, and to wander through the narrow lanes between the houses, visiting the fountain by the river, where Grey Wagtail can be seen.

Turn back along the 124 eastwards and just before reaching Salir turn north, where it is signed to Alcaria and Rocha da Pena. The road has been upgraded and is most scenic winding up through the hills of Cork and Scrub Oak, cistus, gorse and broom, although some have been cleared for agriculture. A diversion to Rocha de Pena can be rewarding, as this is a hill of 479m with Dartford and Subalpine Warblers. Then return to the road at Alcaria and continue up through the little villages. Along the route stop at likely places where some of the previous mentioned birds can be found, such as the woodpeckers, Short-toed Treecreepers and even Olivaceous Warbler.

Plate 9. *Small groups of Greater Flamingo use the saltpans for resting and feeding at Fuseta.*

Plate 10. *Marshes and estuary at Tavira. At low tide the haunt of innumerable waders. A good area for Curlew Sandpiper, Redshank, Spotted Redshank, Little Stint, Turnstone and Oystercatchers.*

Plate 11. *Monte Gordo Stone pine woodlands are within easy walking distance of the town, with a number of tracks running through them. The habitat of a small number of Azure-winged Magpie, Short-toed Treecreeper, Crested Tits and Shrikes found in the woods.*

Plate 12. *Serra de Mú au de Caldeirão showing the gum cistus undergrowth beneath the cork and scrub oaks. Olivaceous, Dartford and Subalpine Warblers inhabit this vegetation with woodpeckers and Crested Tits in the trees.*

Plate 13. *Silves, once the capital of the Algarve with an ancient castle and church. Pallid and Alpine Swifts nest amongst the Swifts. A few Lesser Kestrel can be found in the old buildings.*

Plate 14. *Serra de Mú au de Caldeirão with the woodland cleared near the river ford. Black-eared Wheatear, Tawny Pipit, Wood, Crested and Thekla Lark inhabit the grassland, with Crested Tit, Woodpeckers and Azure-winged Magpie in the trees.*

After Malhão, the road eventually dips down to a small river crossing the road. From here the road becomes gravel. A picnic at this river ford will be rewarded by Azure-winged Magpies drinking and bathing in the stream with Goldfinch, Serins, Greenfinches and Linnets slaking their thirst. At this point there are tracks running along the streams, worth examining on foot. Be careful not to block them, as they are used by farm vehicles.

Grey Wagtails fly up and down the river, whilst Melodious Warbler, Nightingale and Cetti's Warbler nest in the vegetation near the river.

Wood Lark and Crested Lark are present on the hillsides. Crested Tits can easily be seen in the trees along with Green and Great Spotted Woodpeckers, and possibly Redstarts and Hawfinch. Black-eared Wheatear enjoy the dry hills. Even in winter it is a good place to stop as many of the resident birds use the stream for drinking and bathing.

Booted Eagle

São Brás de Alportel

The road north from São Brás de Alportel, north of Faro, has good woodland, not too deforested. São Brás de Alportel has an excellent pousada, making a good central stopping place away from the coast.

Road 2 north from São Brás de Alportel has large areas of unspoilt Cork and Scrub Oak with typical undergrowth. The road is very winding and scenic. A number of minor roads and tracks lead off, which can be explored with chances of Short-toed Eagle and Booted Eagle, as well as the woodland birds already mentioned.

From São Brás de Alportel to Barranco Velho and back to Loulé makes a good morning drive, or to make a pleasant day's tour, with plenty to see, the road from Barranco Velho the 124, can be continued west to São Bartolomeu de Messines and back down to the coast.

Very little birdwatching has been carried out in Portugal, even in the Algarve, so that further research would be of great value. There are many areas inland from the coast, that have been unexplored for their bird life, and the information would be welcomed by C.E.M.P.A.

The checklist of the birds of the Algarve

The checklist numbers 236 species of bird. The key to the status is very limited, and therefore in some areas more or less of that species may be present at different times of the year.

Very little work has been carried out in the Algarve, and certainly there is no information on bird watching regions. There may well be a number of other rarities passing through on migration. It is strange that amongst the large number of British residents, there appears to be so few interested in ornithology. The authors hope with this booklet pointing out a number of places to birdwatch, it may stimulate more interest.

Portugal has been neglected over the years for it's wildlife, both by the people themselves, although this is improving, and by the visitors. The country has a very varied habitat and even the Algarve which has become a popular holiday area with great coastal development, has interesting areas to visit, and many in the mountains unexplored by birdwatchers.

It would be interesting, for example, to know the status of the Purple Heron that no longer breeds at Ludo.

Visitors records would be much appreciated by C.E.M.P.A.

Centro de Estudos de Migracões E Proteccao de Aves
Serviço de Estudos do Ambiente
Rua da Lapa 73
1200 Lisboa
Portugal

Key to symbols

R = Resident	S = Summer	W = Winter	M = Migrant
rM = Rare migrant	pM = Passage migrant	V = Vagrant	
r = Rare	c = Common	U = Uncommon	I = Introduced

Rock Bunting

	English name	Scientific name	Status
✓	Great Northern Diver	Gavia immer	W, U
	Red-throated Diver	Gavia stellata	W, U
	Great Crested Grebe	Podiceps cristatos	R, r
✓	Black-necked Grebe	Podiceps nigricollis	R, r
✓✓✓	Little Grebe	Tachybaptus ruficollis	R, c
	Manx Shearwater	Puffinus puffinus	W, U
	Cory's Shearwater	Calonectris diomedea	W, U
	Storm Petrel	Hydrobates pelagicus	W, U
✓✓✓	Gannet	Sula bassana	W, U
✓	Shag	Phalacrocorax artistotelis	R, c
✓✓✓	Cormorant	Phalacrocorax carbo	W, c
	Little Bittern	Ixobrychus minutus	S, U
	Night Heron	Nycticorax nycticorax	S, U
✓✓✓	Cattle Egret	Bubulcus ibis	R, c
	Squacco Heron	Ardeola ralloides	S, r
✓✓✓	Little Egret	Egretta garzetta	R, c
✓✓✓	Grey Heron	Ardea cinerea	W, c
	Purple Heron	Ardea purpurea	S, U
	Black Stork	Ciconia nigra	pM, r
✓✓✓	White Stork	Ciconia ciconia	R, c
✓ ✓	Spoonbill	Platalea leucorodia	M, U
	Glossy Ibis	Plegadis falcinellus	V, r
✓✓	Greater Flamingo	Phaenicopterus ruber	W, c
	Greylag Goose	Anser anser	W, U
✓✓	Wigeon	Anas penelope	W, c
✓✓✓	Mallard	Anas platyrhynchos	R, c
✓✓	Gadwall	Anas strepera	W, c
✓	Pintail	Anas acuta	W, c
✓✓✓	Shoveler	Anas clypeata	W, c
✓✓✓	Teal	Anas crecca	W, c
	Pochard	Aythya ferina	W, c
	Tufted Duck	Aythya fuligula	W, c
	Common Scoter	Melanitta nigra	W, U
	Black Kite	Milvus migrans	M, U
	Red Kite	Milvus milvus	R, r
	Montagu's Harrier	Circus pygargus	R, U
	Hen Harrier	Circus cyaneus	W, r
	Marsh Harrier	Circus aervginosus	pM, r
	Sparrowhawk	Accipiter nisus	R, U
	Goshawk	Accipiter gentilis	R, r
	Honey Buzzard	Pernis apivorus	pM, U
✓✓	Buzzard	Buteo buteo	R, c
	Long-legged Buzzard	Buteo rufinus	W, r
	Golden Eagle	Aquila chrysaetos	R, r
	Bonelli's Eagle	Hieraaetus fasciatus	R, U
	Booted Eagle	Hieraaetus pennatus	S, c
	Short-toed Eagle	Circaetus gallicus	S, c
	Osprey	Pandion haliaetus	M, U
✓✓✓	Kestrel	Falco tinnunclus	R, c
	Lesser Kestrel	Falco naumanni	S, U

Barnacle Goose oo
Red-breasted Merganser

44

	English name	Scientific name	Status
	Common Gull	*Larus canus*	W, r
	Kittiwake	*Rissa tridactyla*	W, r
✓ ✓ ✓	Great Black-backed Gull	*Larus marinus*	W, r
✓ ✓ ✓	Lesser Black-backed Gull	*Larus fuscus*	R, c
	Gull-billed Tern	*Gelochelidon nilotica*	W/R? U
✓ ✓ ✓	Sandwich Tern	*Sterna sandvicensis*	W, c
✓	Common Tern	*Sterna hirundo*	pM, U
	Little Tern	*Sterna albifrons*	S, c
✓ ✓ ✓	Caspian Tern	*Sterna caspia*	W, U
	Black Tern	*Chlidonias niger*	pM, U
	Whiskered Tern	*Chlidonias hybridus*	pM, U
	Guillemot	*Uria aalge*	W, U
	Razorbill	*Alca torda*	W, U
	Puffin	*Fratercula arctica*	W, U
	Woodpigeon	*Columba palumbus*	R, c
	Stock Dove	*Columba oenas*	R, r
✓ ✓	Rock Dove	*Columba livia*	R, U
✓ ✓ ✓	Collared Dove	*Streptopelia decaocto*	I, U
	Turtle Dove	*Streptopelia turtur*	S, c
	Cuckoo	*Cuculus canorus*	S, c
	Great Spotted Cuckoo	*Clamator glandarius*	S, U
	Barn Owl	*Tyto alba*	R, U
	Short-eared Owl	*Asio flammeus*	W, U
	Eagle Owl	*Bubo bubo*	R, U
	Tawny Owl	*Strix aluco*	R, c
	Scops Owl	*Otus scops*	S, U
✓ ✓ ✓	Little Owl	*Athene noctua*	R, c
	Nightjar	*Caprimulgus europaeus*	pM, U
	Red-necked Nightjar	*Caprimulgus ruficollis*	S, c
	Alpine Swift	*Apus melba*	S, c
	Pallid Swift	*Apus pallidus*	S, c
	Swift	*Apus apus*	S, c
✓ ✓ ✓	Kingfisher	*Alcedo atthis*	R, c
	Bee-eater	*Merops apiaster*	S, c
	Roller	*Coracias garrulus*	S, r
✓ ✓ ✓	Hoopoe	*Upupa epops*	R, c
	Wryneck	*Jynx torquilla*	S, U
	Green Woodpecker	*Picus viridis*	R, c
✓	Great Spotted Woodpecker	*Dendrocopos major*	R, c
	Lesser Spotted Woodpecker	*Dendrocopos minor*	R, U
	Skylark	*Alauda arvensis*	W/R?, c
✓	Woodlark	*Lullula arborea*	R, c
✓ ✓ ✓	Crested Lark	*Galerida cristata*	R, c
✓ ✓ ✓	Thekla Lark	*Galerida theklae*	R, c
	Short-toed Lark	*Calandrella brachydactyla*	S, c
	Lesser Short-toed Lark	*Calandrella rufescens*	S, r
	Calandra Lark	*Melanocorypha calandra*	R, U
✓ ✓ ✓	Crag Martin	*Ptonoprogne rupestris*	RW, c
	Sand Martin	*Riparia riparia*	S, c
✓	Red-rumped Swallow	*Hirundo daurica*	S, U

45

						English name	Scientific name	Status
						Hobby	*Falco subbuteo*	S, r
						Peregrine	*Falco peregrinus*	R, r
						Merlin	*Falco columbarius*	pM, r
						Red-legged Partridge	*Alectoris rufa*	R, c
						Quail	*Coturnix coturnix*	S, c
						Water Rail	*Rallus aquaticus*	R, c
✓	✓	✓				Moorhen	*Gallinus chloropus*	R, c
✓	✓	✓				Coot	*Fulica atra*	R, c
						Purple Gallinule	*Porphyrio porphyrio*	R, U
						Little Bustard	*Tetrax tetrax*	R, U
✓	✓	✓				Oystercatcher	*Haematopus ostralegus*	W, c
✓	✓	✓				Stone Curlew	*Burhinus oedicnemus*	R, c
✓	✓	✓				Black-winged Stilt	*Himantopus himantopus*	R, c
✓	✓	✓				Avocet	*Recurvirostra avosetta*	R, c
						Collared Partincole	*Glareola pratincola*	S, c
✓	✓	✓				Ringed Plover	*Charadrius hiaticula*	W, c
						Little Ringed Plover	*Charadrius dubius*	S, c
✓	✓	✓				Kentish Plover	*Charadrius alexandrinus*	R, c
	✓	✓				Golden Plover	*Pluvialis apricaria*	W, c
✓	✓	✓				Grey Plover	*Pluvialis squatarola*	W, c
✓	✓	✓				Lapwing	*Vanellus vanellus*	W, c
✓		✓				Turnstone	*Arenaria interpres*	W, c
✓	✓	✓				Sanderling	*Calidris alba*	pM, U
	✓	✓				Knot	*Calidris canutus*	pM, r
						Curlew Sandpiper	*Calidris ferruginea*	pM, U
✓	✓	✓				Dunlin	*Calidris alpina*	W, c
						Purple Sandpiper	*Calidris maritima*	W, r
✓						Little Stint	*Calidris minuta*	pM, U
						Ruff	*Philomachus pugnax*	pM, U
✓	✓	✓				Curlew	*Numenius arquata*	pM, c
✓		✓				Whimbrel	*Numenius phaeopus*	pM, c
✓	✓	✓				Black-tailed Godwit	*Limosa limosa*	W, c
		✓				Bar-tailed Godwit	*Limosa lapponica*	pM, U
✓	✓	✓				Redshank	*Tringa totanus*	W, c
✓	✓	✓				Greenshank	*Tringa nebularia*	pM, c
✓						Spotted Redshank	*Tringa erythropus*	pM, c
						Wood Sandpiper	*Tringa glareola*	pM, r
	✓					Green Sandpiper	*Tringa ochropus*	pM, r
✓	✓	✓				Common Sandpiper	*Actitis hypoleucos*	W/R?, c
						Woodcock	*Scolopax rusticola*	W, U
	✓					Snipe	*Gallingo gallingo*	W, c
						Jack Snipe	*Lymnocryptes minimus*	W, r
						Great Skua	*Stercorarius skua*	W, r
						Pomerine Skua	*Stercorarius pomarinus*	W, r
						Arctic Skua	*Stercorarius parasticus*	W, r
✓						Mediterranean Gull	*Larus melanocephalus*	W, U
						Slender-billed Gull	*Larus genei*	W, r
						Little Gull	*Larus minutus*	W, U
✓	✓	✓				Black-headed Gull	*Larus ridibundus*	W, c
✓	✓	✓				Herring Gull	*Larus argentatus*	R, c

✓   *March sdpr*

46

						English name	Scientific name	Status
✓	✓					Swallow	*Hirundo rustica*	S, c
✓	✓					House Martin	*Delichon urbica*	S, c
✓	✓					Rock Pipit	*Anthus petrosus*	W, U
✓		✓				Water Pipit	*Anthus spinoletta*	W, U
	✓					Meadow Pipit	*Anthus pratensis*	W, c
						Tawny Pipit	*Anthus campestris*	S, U
✓	✓	✓				Pied Wagtail	*Motacilla alba*	WR, c
✓	✓	✓				Grey Wagtail	*Motacilla cinerea*	R, c
						Yellow Wagtail	*Motacilla flava iberiae*	S, c
	✓					Wren	*Troglodytes troglodytes*	R, c
						Dunnock	*Prunella modularis*	W, U
						Alpine Accentor	*Prunella collaris*	W, r
✓	✓	✓				Robin	*Erithacus rubecula*	R, c
						Nightingale	*Luscinia megarhynchos*	S, c
						Rufous Bush Robin	*Cerotrichas galactotes*	S, U
✓	✓	✓				Bluethroat	*Luscinia svecica cyanecula*	W, U
						Redstart	*Phoenicurus phoenicurus*	S, U
✓	✓	✓				Black Redstart	*Phoenicurus ochruros*	R, c
						Whinchat	*Saxicola rubetra*	pM, U
✓	✓	✓				Stonechat	*Saxicola torquata*	R, c
						Wheatear	*Oenanthe oenanthe*	pM, U
						Black-eared Wheatear	*Oenanthe hispanica*	S, c
						Rock Thrush	*Monticola saxitilis*	pM, U
	✓					Blue Rock Thrush	*Monticola solitarius*	R, U
						Ring Ouzel	*Turdus torquatus*	W, r
✓	✓	✓				Blackbird	*Turdus merula*	R, c
						Fieldfare	*Turdus pilaris*	W, U
						Redwing	*Turdus iliacus*	W, U
	✓					Song Thrush	*Turdus philomelos*	W, c
						Mistle Thrush	*Turdus viscivorus*	R, c
✓	✓	✓				Fan-tailed Warbler	*Cisticola juncidis*	R, c
						Cetti's Warbler	*Cettia cetti*	R, c
						Great Reed Warbler	*Acrocephalus arundinaceus*	S, c
						Reed Warbler	*Acrocephalus scirpaceus*	S, U
						Sedge Warbler	*Acrocephalus schoenobaenus*	W, r
						Olivaceous Warbler	*Hippolais pallida*	S, r
						Melodius Warbler	*Hippolais polyglotta*	S, c
✓	✓					Dartford Warbler	*Sylvia undata*	R, c
						Subalpine Warbler	*Sylvia cantillans*	S, U
						Spectacled Warbler	*Sylvia conspicillata*	S, U
						Garden Warbler	*Sylvia borin*	pM, U
						Whitethroat	*Sylvia communis*	S, U
✓	✓	✓				Blackcap	*Sylvia atricapilla*	R, c
✓	✓	✓				Sardinian Warbler	*Sylvia melanocephala*	R, c
						Orphean Warbler	*Sylvia hortensis*	S, r
						Bonelli's Warbler	*Phylloscopus bonelli*	pM/R? U
✓						Willow Warbler	*Phylloscopus trochilus*	pM, r
✓	✓	✓				Chiffchaff	*Phylloscopus collybita*	W, c
						Goldcrest	*Regulus regulus*	W, r
						Firecrest	*Regulus ignicapillus*	W/R? U

✓✓✓ Tree Pipit

47

						English name	Scientific name	Status
						Spotted Flycatcher	*Muscicapa striata*	S, U
						Penduline Tit	*Remiz pendulinus*	W, r
						Crested Tit	*Parus cristatus*	R, c
✓						Blue Tit	*Parus caeruleus*	R, c
✓	✓	✓				Great Tit	*Parus major*	R, c
						Long-tailed Tit	*Aeithalos caudatus*	R, c
						Nuthatch	*Sitta europaea*	R, c
						Short-toed Treecreeper	*Certhia brachydactyla*	R, c
✓	✓					Great Grey Shrike	*Lanius excubitor*	R, c
						Woodchat Shrike	*Lanius senator*	S, c
						Starling	*Sturnus vulgaris*	W, U
✓	✓	✓				Spotless Starling	*Sturnus unicolor*	R, c
						Golden Oriole	*Oriolus oriolus*	S, c
✓						Jay	*Garrulus glandarius*	R, c
✓	✓	✓				Azure-winged Magpie	*Cyanopica cyana*	R, c
						Chough	*Pyrrhocorax pyrrhocorax*	R, U
✓	✓	✓				Jackdaw	*Corvus monedula*	R, c
						Raven	*Corvus corax*	R, U
						Crow	*Corvus corone*	R, U
						Tree Sparrow	*Passer montanus*	R, U
✓	✓	✓				House Sparrow	*Passer domesticus*	R, c
						Rock Sparrow	*Petronia petronia*	R, U
✓						Common Waxbill	*Estrilda astrild*	I, c
✓	✓	✓				Chaffinch	*Fringilla coelebs*	R, c
						Brambling	*Fringilla montifringilla*	W, r
						Hawfinch	*Coccothraustes coccothraustes*	R, U
✓	✓	✓				Serin	*Serinus serinus*	R, c
✓	✓					Siskin	*Carduelis spinus*	W, r
✓	✓	✓				Greenfinch	*Carduelis chloris*	R, c
✓	✓	✓				Goldfinch	*Carduelis carduelis*	R, c
						Bullfinch	*Pyrrhula pyrrhula*	W, r
✓	✓	✓				Linnet	*Carduelis cannabina*	R, c
✓	✓					Corn Bunting	*Miliaria calandra*	R, c
						Cirl Bunting	*Emberiza cirlus*	R, c
						Rock Bunting	*Emberiza cia*	R, c
						Reed Bunting	*Emberiza schoeniclus*	W, r
✓						Temminck's Stint ✓		
	✓					Gr white Egret.		
83	✓					Spanish Sparrow		

48

							English name	Scientific name	Status

NOTES

Orphean Warbler

NOTES

NOTES